173.3
L

Cities of the Revolution

NEW YORK

By Susan & John Lee

Illustrated by Ralph Canaday

 CHILDRENS PRESS, CHICAGO

Library of Congress Cataloging in Publication Data

Lee, Susan.
  New York.

  (Cities of the Revolution)
  SUMMARY: Simple text and illustrations describe
the history of New York City from its founding by the
Dutch through the Revolutionary War.
  1. New York (City)—History—Revolution, 1775-
1783—Juvenile literature. [1. New York (City)—
History—Colonial period, ca. 1600-1775. 2. New York
(City)—History—Revolution, 1775-1783] I. Canaday,
Ralph, ill. II. Title.
F128.44.L55   974.7′1′03   74-26649
ISBN 0-516-04686-1

3 4 5 6 7 8 9 10 11 12 R 78 77 76

CONTENTS

In OUR REVOLUTIONARY WAR . . . the English soldier was like a boy who knows how to fight. He knows how to move his feet. He knows how to hold his hands. He has won many fights and knows he is a good fighter.

The American soldier was like a boy who does not know much about fighting. He doesn't know how to move. He isn't sure what to do. He hasn't been hit hard. And he doesn't know what he will do when he is hit.

This book tells part of the story of how General Washington's soldiers learned to fight—in New York.

Chapter 1

THE DUTCH OF
NEW AMSTERDAM

The first white men came to Manhattan in April, 1524. Captain da Verrazano was exploring for the King of France. He wrote about the "steep little hills" and the "great stream of water." Later, the hills were called Brooklyn Heights and the river was the Hudson.

The first black man came to Manhattan in January, 1526. Estaban Gomez was exploring for the King of Spain. The next explorer was Henry Hudson, who sailed for the Dutch. In September, 1609, Hudson sailed up the "great stream" and traded for furs with the Indians.

The Dutch came back the next year, 1610, for more furs. They called this land New Netherland after their home country. Three years later the Dutch built a little fort, 36 feet long and 26 feet wide, up the river. Fur trading was good business for the Dutch. They started the Dutch West Indies Company. It had three jobs. One was to capture Spanish ships loaded with gold. One was to build up the fur trade with Indians. One was to start a colony in New Netherland.

A large ship, the *New Netherland*, brought 110 men, women, and children to the new land. The trip from the Netherlands to Manhattan took almost two months. The ship got to Manhattan in May of 1623.

Two families and six men went to what is now the Hartford River in Connecticut. Two families and eight men went to what is now the Delaware River. Eight men stayed on Manhattan. The rest

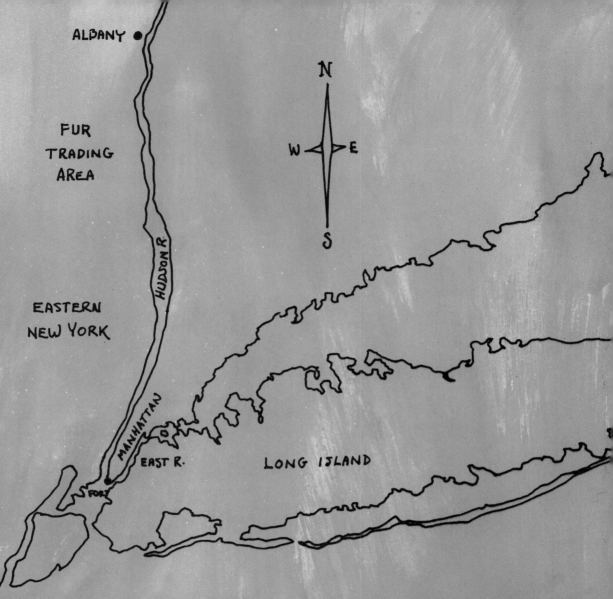

of the families went up the North (Hudson)
River. The old fort was gone so they built a new
one. They called it Fort Orange; today we call
the place Albany.

The eight men on Manhattan moved to a small island covered with nut trees. Then 45 more colonists came to join them. These colonists had horses, cows, hogs, and sheep with them. There wasn't much water on Nut Island, so the group moved over to Manhattan in 1624.

The men who led the Dutch were called
directors. The third director was Peter Minuit. In
May, 1626, Minuit met with the Indian chiefs
who lived on and near the island. Minuit gave
the Indians 60 guilders (forty dollars) worth of

cloth, beads, and other trade goods. The Indians traded the island for this pile of junk.

The Dutch lived at the south end of the island. On the west side, along the North River, were the company farm and orchard. On the east side, along the East River, were many small houses and farms. Most of the island was covered with oak, maple, pine, and other trees. There were many kinds of animals—deer, bear, even mountain lions.

Over the next 20 years, more and more Dutch came to the island. Each family had a small farm. They had many cattle and pigs and chickens. They grew corn and wheat on the farms.

The Indians were good trappers. They trapped animals and sold the furs to the Dutch. The little town was a center of trade. There was some fighting with Indians. When fighting started the farmers went into the fort.

Some English families moved onto Long Island. Some English moved onto land north of Manhattan Island. The Dutch and English got along without fighting.

In 1646, Peter Stuyvesant became governor of the Dutch colony. Ten years later there were 1,000 people and 120 houses around the fort. The Dutch called the little city New Amsterdam.

Two cowpaths led out of the fort. One went north through the farms. It had been an old

Indian trail. The Dutch called it Heere Street
(High Street). Today it is called Broadway, one
of the best-known streets in the world. The other
path went along the shore of the East River.
Today it is called Pearl Street.

The Dutch colony was a good place for
farming and trading. The farm lands had very
rich soil. The rivers made a good harbor for
ships.

Governor Stuyvesant had a wall built from one side of the island to the other. There were two gates in the wall so people and cattle could go in and out. The wall was to keep the Indians out in case of war. But when war came, it was with the English.

In 1664, the English sent four ships to the island. The Dutch didn't want to fight. They gave up. The Englishman who took the city was the Duke of York. He named the colony New York. He also gave his name to New York City.

There were two more wars between the Dutch and the English. The Dutch got the city back once. But in the end, they lost both wars. So England owned the colony of New York.

The Dutch stayed in New York City. But most new colonists were English. The two groups got along without much trouble.

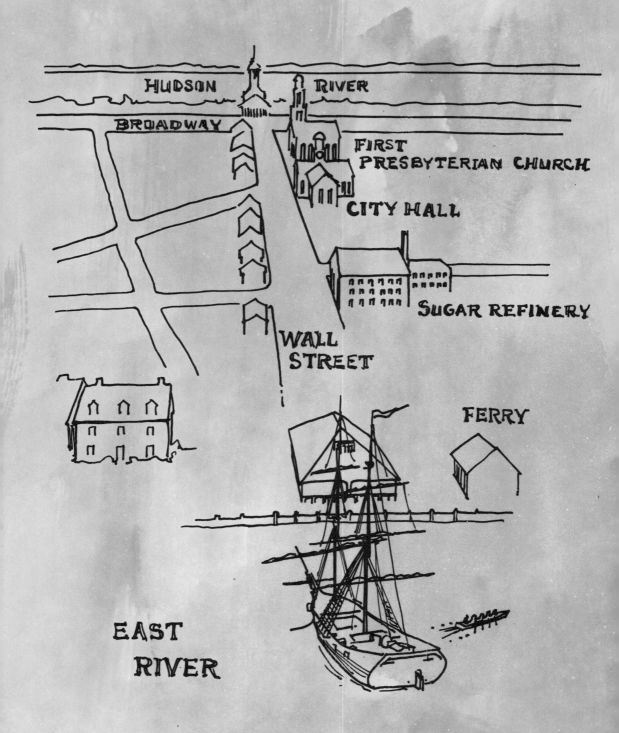

HUDSON RIVER

BROADWAY

FIRST PRESBYTERIAN CHURCH

CITY HALL

SUGAR REFINERY

WALL STREET

FERRY

EAST RIVER

18

Chapter 2

THE ENGLISH
OF NEW YORK

By 1734, there were about 10,000 people in New York City. Most of them were white, but there were many black slaves. New York City was a growing harbor town. There were farms on the island, up the Hudson, and in New Jersey. These farms grew wheat. The wheat was sent to New York City and ground into flour. From the city, it was shipped to England and to the West Indies.

At this time, most of the big colonial cities were on rivers or bays by the ocean. People got from place to place by boat or ship. There were no good roads, just old paths the Indians had used.

A good harbor was very important. Ships could get to the city from England. Ships could come and go to other colonies. Farmers who lived along the rivers could send their crops down the river to the harbor. A good harbor and rich farmlands would make a city grow in many ways.

There are many ways to earn money in a trading city. Someone has to build ships. Someone has to buy the ships. Someone has to sail the ships.

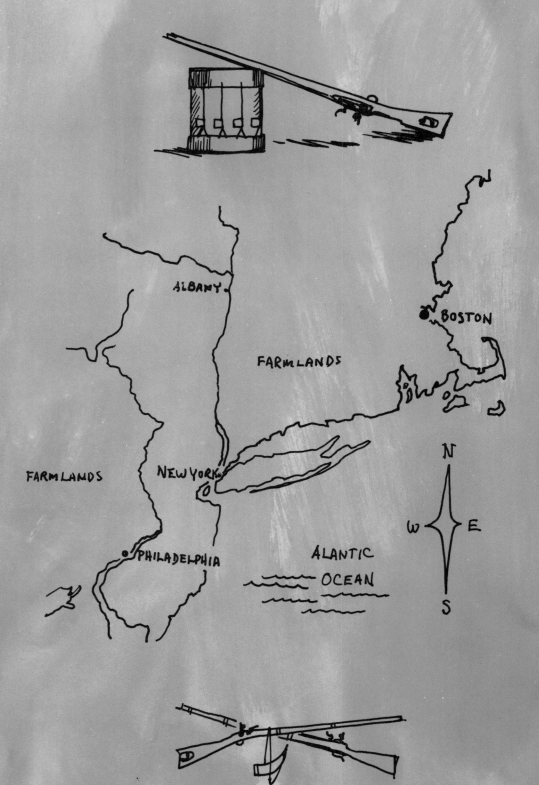

ALBANY

FARMLANDS

BOSTON

FARMLANDS

NEW YORK

PHILADELPHIA

ALANTIC
OCEAN

N

W   E

S

The farmer earns money for his wheat. The miller earns money for making flour. Someone earns money for storing the flour in his warehouse. Someone earns money for loading flour on the ships.

Most of the New York flour was shipped to England. There it was unloaded and sold. Bakers would buy the flour. They would sell bread and cakes in their stores.

The English would send clothing and tools and guns back to New York City. The English earned money making these things. In this way trade was good for England and her colonies.

By 1734, trade had made New York City one of the biggest colonial cities. Wall Street was, even then, an important street.

A ferry ran from New York City to Long Island. There was a big Meal Market (flour and corn). This market was also used for selling and buying slaves. There was a sugar factory.

The City Hall was a big building. In it were courtrooms, juryrooms, and a jail. The library and the fire department were also in it.

There were two big churches on Wall Street. There were coffee houses, taverns, and stores. There were many fine homes on the street.

Some of New York's streets were paved. Round stones were used. The middle of the streets were dirt. There was a ditch in the dirt so rainwater would run off.

In those days people threw their garbage into the streets. The pigs and dogs would eat the

garbage. The chickens and pigeons got many a good meal out on the streets.

There were wells and pumps on most of the streets of New York City. This water was used for cooking, drinking, and washing. Most of the city's water did not taste very good. The best water came from the Tea Water Pump. The wells and pumps were also used to help fight fires.

There were no schools as we know them. But there were teachers. Boys and girls would go to a teacher's house. They would learn to read and write and count.

There were also teachers for music and singing. There was a college—King's College. Some rich people sent their children to school in England.

New York City was a good place for colonists to live. There were many ways to earn money in the city.

It was a safe place to live. There were no
Indians on the island. There was a time when
many pirates lived in the city. Captain William
Kidd had owned three houses there. But the
people had gotten rid of the pirates. There was
no trouble in the city for years. People were too
busy making money to make trouble.

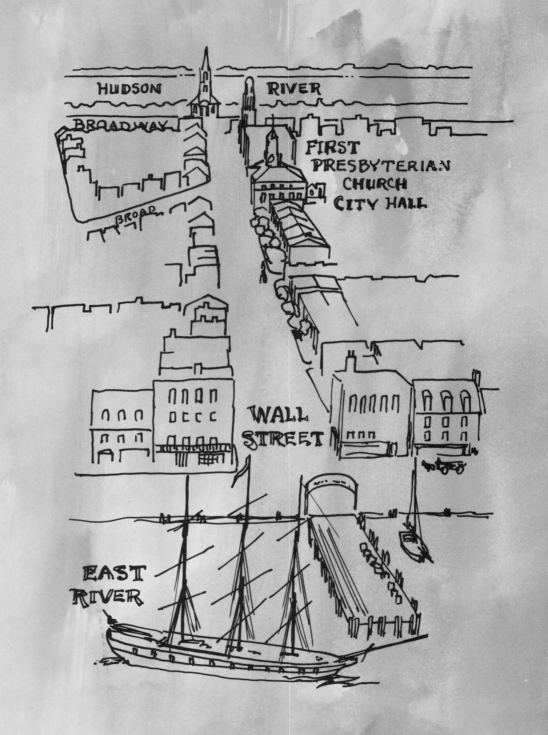

HUDSON RIVER

BROADWAY

BROAD

FIRST
PRESBYTERIAN
CHURCH
CITY HALL

WALL
STREET

EAST
RIVER

28

Chapter 3

REBELS AND LOYALISTS

Each year New York City grew larger. More and more people came to the city. More and more houses and stores were built to the north of the city.

Look at the first picture of Wall Street. Now look at this picture. You can see for yourself how the city changed over 40 years.

Long Island also grew in the same ways. Brooklyn was the main city on that island. The island had many good farms.

The colony of New York belonged to England. A governor from England lived in New York City. He ran the colony for the King of England.

The King ruled all the English people. Most of the English lived in England. Some of the English lived in colonies in America and other parts of the world.

The members of Parliament made laws for all the people under English rule. Most members of Parliament were elected by the English who lived in England. The people in the English colonies did not get to vote for members of Parliament.

The colonies in America were a long way from England. Many of the colonists had been born in the colonies. They had never seen England or their King. They had never seen a member of Parliament. They had begun to think of themselves as both Americans and English.

The trouble between the colonies and England began over taxes and trade. The English needed money so they taxed the colonies. The Americans said this wasn't fair. There weren't any members of Parliament from America.

There was a lot of talk about taxes and rights by both sides. But it was just talk until the Americans said they wouldn't pay the taxes.

One of the taxes was on paper. All paper used for business had to have a special stamp. This tax was called the Stamp Act. The Americans would not buy the stamps. They beat up some of the men who had the job of selling stamps. They burned many stamps.

The Tea Act was a law that gave one group of English the right to sell tea. This group raised the price of tea. They didn't raise the price a little. They raised it a lot.

The Americans didn't like this. They wanted to buy tea at a low price. They said they had the right to buy tea from anyone. The English said they had to buy from one special group of traders.

In New York there was a group of Americans called the Sons of Liberty. In 1774, the Sons of Liberty had a tea party.

The Sons of Liberty went onto an English ship in New York Harbor. They threw all the English tea into the East River. This same sort of thing happened in other American cities.

In April, 1775, an American rode into New

York City. Israel Bessel came down Broadway and turned onto Wall Street. The churches had just let out and the street was full of people.

Bessel had ridden from Boston with news. The English and Americans had fought at Concord and Lexington. The English army had pulled back into Boston. The Americans had put their army around Boston.

The Sons of Liberty took over City Hall. The English had 500 guns stored there. For a week no one—not the English, not the Americans—ran New York City. Then on May 1, the Americans took over the government of the city.

At this time, there were three main groups in New York City. There were colonists who were loyal to King George and to England. They were called loyalists, and they were willing to help the English soldiers.

There were colonists who wanted to be free of England. They were willing to fight the English in the name of freedom. They were called American rebels.

There were colonists who didn't want to fight at all. They weren't mad at anyone. They just wanted to be left alone to farm or to trade.

When the rebels took over, some of the loyalists were beaten or whipped. Many loyalists left the city. Most of the people who didn't want to fight stayed. They pretended to be rebels.

On July 4, 1776, the Declaration of Independence was signed. General Washington was in New York City when the news came on July 9. The Declaration of Independence was read to the army and the people. They shot off guns. They had a parade. They tore down the statue of King George and made over 42,000 lead bullets from it.

War was about to come to New York City.

Chapter 4

THE BATTLES
AROUND NEW YORK

In the fall of 1776, 130 English ships sailed into New York Harbor. Then 150 more ships came to New York. There were 32,000 men in the English army. It was the biggest army ever seen in the Americas.

The English moved onto Staten Island. For a month they were quiet. The English generals did not want a war. They didn't want anyone to fight or die. They hoped their big army would scare the Americans. They hoped the colonies would stay loyal to King George.

General Washington put 4,000 American
soldiers outside Brooklyn. In August, the English
put 20,000 men on Long Island. Washington
sent 3,000 more men to Brooklyn.

The battle of Long Island lasted just one day.
The English army was too good for the
Americans. By night, all the Americans had been
driven back into Brooklyn.

Washington was in a bad spot. He was sure to lose his army when the English attacked again. Then came a lucky night of hard rain and fog. The Americans got all the small boats they could find. They rowed from Brooklyn to New York City. The boats went back and forth all night. The English woke up to find the Americans gone. Washington had lost a battle. But he had saved his army.

King George and the English were happy with the news of the battle. The English said it would be a short war. They said their army could beat any other army in the world.

The Americans were sad about the battle. Their army had lost. Many men left the army and went home. The American generals knew the English could take New York anytime.

The American Congress told Washington to stay on Manhattan. They told him to stay and fight. Washington didn't think this was a good idea. But he and his army stayed to fight.

Washington put most of his men on some high ground called Harlem Heights. They were at the north end of the island. There were 3,000 American soldiers in New York City.

In September, the English landed on Manhattan. They came in at Kip's Bay. They drove off the few Americans at the bay. Then the English moved in and took the Boston Post Road.

This was the only big road from the city to the north end of the island. The English had trapped the 3,000 soldiers in New York City. If they could beat Washington it might be the end of the war.

The Americans moved out of the city on little farm roads. Then they moved north on Bloomingdale Road. They moved as fast as they could. The English moved north on the Boston Post Road. They moved slowly. Only a thick woods kept the two armies from seeing each other. It was mostly luck that the Americans got to Harlem Heights first. They were out of the trap.

Washington had about 10,000 soldiers. The English had about 13,000. The English had won on Long Island and at Kip's Bay. The Americans had begun to think they couldn't beat the English army.

Washington sent 100 rangers down the hill to hit the English line. The English attacked. The rangers fell back. The English went after them. This time Washington trapped the English. His men hit the English from the side. The men who had lost on Long Island now stopped the English.

Then Washington sent in the men who had lost at Kip's Bay. They drove the English back.

The Americans had beaten the best English soldiers.

This small battle meant a lot to the Americans. They had won. The same American soldiers who were beaten before had beaten the well-trained English soldiers. The Americans now knew the English were just men, not supermen.

Chapter 5

THE ENGLISH WIN
NEW YORK CITY

The English did not attack the Americans again. Part of the English army moved into New York City. They used City Hall as a jail for rebels. They used the churches as hospitals. The officers moved into the best houses.

In September, 1776, a great fire swept the city. Most of the houses along Broadway were burned. The west side of the city was ruined. The English said the rebels set the fire. The rebels were put in jail or left the city.

The English army sailed to Westchester, north of Manhattan. Washington moved most of his army to Westchester. In October the two armies fought at White Plains. Later, Washington moved his army across the Hudson River. He took the army into New Jersey. New York was now English. It stayed an English city until the end of the war.

For over six years, the English held New York City. The loyalists came back. The rebels were gone. The English used the city badly. They didn't take care of the houses they used. They cut down trees for firewood. They didn't build anything new. The streets were full of garbage. In a way, New York was a dying city.

The last big battle of the war was fought at Yorktown in 1781. It took two years for the Americans and English to work out a peace treaty. The English army stayed in New York until 1783. Before the army left, over 7,000 loyalists sailed from New York. Some of them went to Canada. Some went to England.

The Americans marched in as the English left. The American parade moved west on Wall Street. Then it went south on Broadway. The city was a mess. The streets were dirty and full of hogs. Houses had to be rebuilt. City Hall was not fit to use. The first American mayor took over the city at a tavern.

In 1784, the American Congress said it would meet in New York City. People began to build new houses and fix up old ones. Stores were built or fixed up. Trade began to pick up. There were jobs for more and more people.

By 1785, New York City was a good place to live again. Wall Street was the most important street in America. Many people came to visit the city.

In 1789, Federal Hall was built for Congress. Washington became President of the United States. New York City was the capital city of all the states. The little Dutch town had become a great American city.

Today New York City is one of the largest, richest cities in the world. It is a center of trade and banking. The 60 guilders spent by the Dutch was one of the great buys of all times.

AUTHOR'S NOTES:

Netherland means low land, land by the sea. The King of Spain owned the Netherland in the 1500s. Later part of the Netherland, called Holland, became a free country, The people of Holland were called the Dutch. The other part of Netherland was Belgium. Many of the Dutch colonists who came to Manhattan were really Belgians, or Walloons as they were called then.

The old Dutch fort is now 39 Broadway. The Dutch filled in part of the East River to get more land. The old shore was where Pearl Street is now. In the early days the East River flowed where Water Street, Front Street, and State Street now stand.

Bouwerie meant farm. There were six Dutch farms on each side of the Bowery. Wall Street really was a wall. First it was a wall of tree stumps. Then it was a wall of logs buried three feet in the ground and standing nine feet above the ground. The wall, from river to river, was 2,340 feet long. Four blocks north of Wall Street a path ran along a little stream. Dutch girls, or maidens, washed their clothes in the stream. Today the path is called Maiden Lane.

What used to be Kip's Bay is now the east end of 34th Street. The woods between the Boston Post Road and Bloomingdale Road is now Central Park. Harlem Heights is still known by that name. The place where the United Nations buildings stand used to be a tobacco field. Barnard College is built on what used to be a wheat field.

The word Manhattan was first written by a mate on Henry Hudson's *Half Moon*. Harlem was once New Haarlem, named after the city of Haarlem in Holland. Jonas Bronck once owned the land where the Bronx is now. Brooklyn began at a place called *Vlacke Bos* (Flatbush). Lady Deborah Moody, an Englishwoman, paid one blanket, one kettle, some beads, three guns, and three pounds of gunpowder for part of Long Island. Her land included what is now Coney Island. The Dutch paid the Indians five times for Staten Island.

The Hudson River had many names. Verrazano called it the Vendome. Gomez called it the San Antonio. Hudson called it Mauritus. The Dutch called it the North River. The English called it the Hudson. The Hudson is now as dirty as the streets of old New York used to be.

SOME DATES . . . . SOME FACTS

1628	Jonas Michaeluis was the first Dutch minister. Adam Roelandsen was the first teacher. His pay was two beaverskins for each pupil. He had so few pupils that he took in washing to make a living. The first brick kiln was built in this year.
1630	The first large ship was built. She was called the *New Netherland* and had 30 cannon.
1633	The Dutch sent 104 soldiers to Manhattan. The first church was built where 39 Pearl Street is now. A brewery was built just east of the Bowery.
1643	The first Catholic priest, Father Jogues, visited the town.

1648	The first pier (dock) was built on the East River.
1652	The first Latin School was opened. The teacher was paid $100 a year. A sailor was paid $96 a year. The first law against fast driving was passed.
1653	A prison was built inside the fort. The city of New Amsterdam got its own government. The five-story tavern at 71-73 Pearl Street became the first City Hall.
1654	The first Jew, Jacob Barsimon, came from Holland. The first Thanksgiving was held on August 12, 1654. The people drank 58 guilders of free beer.
1655	The first school was built from money earned at the city tavern.
1656	The first market was built at Pearl and Whitehall Streets.
1657	The fire department was started with money from a tax on chimneys.
1658	The first public well was dug. The first policemen were hired. In this year, a horse cost $112, an ox cost $48, and a slave cost $280.
1659	The first hospital was built on Bridge Street.
1660	The first post office was opened.
1663	The first earthquake shook the town.
1664	Duke of York reaches Manhattan. Dutch surrender. English rule begins.
1665	City is renamed New York.

1664-67	English and Dutch fight second war.
1673-74	English and Dutch fight third war. Dutch lose.
1678	New York City given monopoly on flour exports. Trade increases.
1732	Bowling Green, the first park, opens.
1734	Ferry runs between city and Long Island.
1762	Slave market closes. Street lights introduced.
1765	Stamp Act Congress. Riots in the city.
1770	Boston Massacre. Anti-English feelings grow.
1774	Sons of Liberty dump tea in New York Harbor.
1775	Lexington and Concord. Rebels take over government of New York City.
1776	Declaration of Independence signed. English win Battle for Long Island . . . Americans win at the Battle of Harlem Heights. Fire destroys part of the city. English army takes over city government.
1779-80	Winters are so bad the bay freezes. All trees cut down for firewood.
1781	Battle of Yorktown.
1783	Peace treaty is signed. English army leaves city.
1784	Congress meets in city. James Duane becomes city's first American mayor.
1789	Federal Hall is built. Washington becomes president. The city is the capital of the United States.

About the Authors:

Susan Dye Lee has been writing professionally since she graduated from college in 1961. Working with the Social Studies Curriculum Center at Northwestern University, she has created course materials in American studies. Ms. Lee has also co-authored a text on Latin America and Canada, written case studies in legal history for the Law in American Society Project, and developed a teacher's guide for tapes that explore women's role in America's past. The writer credits her students for many of her ideas. Currently, she is doing research for her history dissertation on the Women's Christian Temperance Union for Northwestern University. In her free moments, Susan Lee enjoys traveling, playing the piano, and welcoming friends to "Highland Cove," the summer cottage she and her husband, John, share.

John R. Lee enjoys a prolific career as a writer, teacher, and outdoorsman. After receiving his doctorate in social studies at Stanford, Dr. Lee came to Northwestern University's School of Education, where he advises student teachers and directs graduates in training. A versatile writer, Dr. Lee has co-authored the Scott-Foresman social studies textbooks for primary-age children. In addition, he has worked on the production of 50 films and over 100 film-strips. His biographical film on Helen Keller received a 1970 Venice Film Festival award. His college text, *Teaching Social Studies in the Elementary School*, has recently been published. Besides pro-football, Dr. Lee's passion is his Wisconsin cottage, where he likes to shingle leaky roofs, split wood, and go sailing.

About the Artist:

Ralph Canaday has been involved in all aspects of commercial art since graduation from the Art Institute of Chicago in 1959. As an illustrator, designer and sculptor his work has appeared in many national publications, textbooks, and corporate promotional material.

He is currently working on his "Famous Aviators" series, a collection of life-size bronze busts in limited edition of such aviators as the Baron Von Richthofen, Charles Lindbergh, Eddie Rickenbacker and Amelia Earhart. His knowledge of aviation history garnered through years of collecting, reading and flying have made him an "expert" in this area. He is also continually working on his aviation illustrations which are a natural adjunct to his "hobby". Ralph lives in Hanover Park, Illinois with his wife Arlene, who is also in publishing.